1.0   Introduction

Hydropower is a primary renewable source of electricity in the United States. Balancing the use of water for the production of electricity and the health of fish populations is an ongoing effort, particularly in the Pacific Northwest.

In the Columbia River hydropower system, downstream migrating fish have three primary alternatives for passing dams: they can 1) go through the turbines, 2) be diverted from the turbines by bypass screens located in the turbine intakes and be redirected into specially designed facilities that allow them to be transported or diverted into the tailrace downstream of the dam, or 3) pass over the dam through spillways and sluiceways.

When fish pass dams, particularly through turbines (Figure 1.1) or in spill (Figure 1.2), they are exposed to severe hydraulic conditions and may be injured or killed (Bell and DeLacy 1972; Bell 1981; Čada et al. 1997; McEwen and Scobie 1992; Monten 1985; Pavlov et al. 1999; Ruggles and Murray 1983; R2 Resource Consultants 1998; Turnpenny et al. 1992; Turnpenny 1998). Injury mechanisms include striking or scraping stationary structures such as turbine wicket gates or spillway stilling basin baffle blocks; being struck by moving elements such as the blades of turbine runners; and getting pinched in

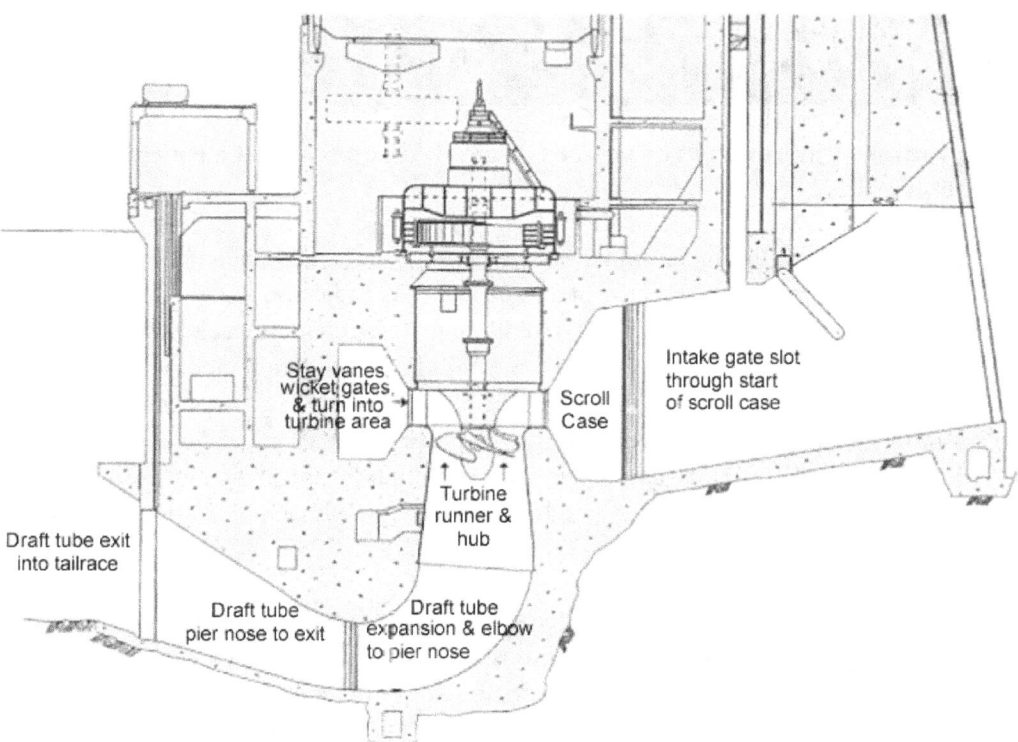

Figure 1.1.   Cross-Section of a Typical Columbia River Federal Hydropower System Kaplan Turbine

Figure 1.2. **Tailrace Environment of Lower Granite Dam on the Snake River During Spill Operations**

gaps at the tips and hub of the turbine's runner blades. Pressure, shear, turbulence, and cavitation can also cause injury or delayed mortality (Abernethy et al. 2001, 2002; Čada et al. 1997; Carlson 2000; Neitzel et al. 2000; Wittinger et al. 1995; Turnpenny 1998). Although consequences such as mortality or visible external injury are quite clearly not good for fish, more subtle effects like temporary disability, stunning or disorientation, are known to make fish more susceptible to predation by birds and other fish as they exit the turbine draft tubes and move downstream in the powerhouse tailrace. When the effects of passage on a fish are studied, particularly mortality, a distinction is made between mortality resulting directly from passage and the mortality that is indirectly linked to passage through predation on fish with reduced function following passage.

Owners and operators of hydropower facilities are seeking to optimize the survival of fish passing dams by redesigning aspects of hydroelectric facilities and their operation. To develop more "fish-friendly" dams, designers need to understand dangers to fish during passage. To get this information, it is necessary to characterize the conditions fish experience when they pass through complex hydraulic environments and identify the locations and operations where conditions are severe enough to injure fish.

Dam operators, fishery biologists, and hydro engineers routinely use both physical and computational fluid dynamic (CFD) models to characterize spillway and turbine passage environments. A missing piece in their analysis, however, was the ability to actually measure conditions that occur *in situ*. In 1998, scientists at Pacific Northwest National Laboratory (PNNL) initiated development of an autonomous sensor that could acquire information to help characterize the conditions fish experience during passage. The result of this development activity was termed the Sensor Fish.

The first Sensor Fish was created as an internal PNNL development initiative. The roughly fish-size prototype, nicknamed "Flubber Fish," successfully demonstrated proof-of-concept for acquiring complex hydraulic data during turbine passage. The U.S. Department of Energy (DOE) Advanced Hydropower Turbine System (AHTS) Program took an interest in the prototype as related to their goal to increase survival of fish passing turbines and has since sponsored ongoing development activities.

The "Flubber Fish" underwent major transformations in 2000 and again in 2002, providing an upgraded sensor package for deployment and rapid retrieval of data. The new product, the Sensor Fish device, has been field tested at Bonneville, McNary, The Dalles, and Rock Island dams on the Columbia River. Sensor Fish devices are deployed in turbines, spillways, and sluiceways to measure changes in pressure and linear acceleration fish experience during dam passage.

Using data collected by the Sensor Fish device during these studies, researchers can better understand what conditions may be responsible for different types of injuries and where these conditions occur during passage. As more studies are conducted using live fish and Sensor Fish, a valuable database that links Sensor Fish time histories with live fish injury and mortality rates is developing. By correlating injuries with specific hydraulic conditions at specific locations in the dam, Sensor Fish can ultimately aid in the design of more fish-friendly dams. The latest Sensor Fish device upgrades have resulted in a device that may be implantable in fish, thereby permitting direct linkage between the injuries a fish may experience during passage through a severe hydraulic environment and the details of their exposure.

This report summarizes the evolution in design of the Sensor Fish device, briefly describes how it works, provides sample data acquired by the device at Columbia River dams, and describes how this information is being used to assess conditions downstream migrant fish might experience as they pass hydroelectric facilities.

2.0   Sensor Fish Design History

The Sensor Fish has undergone significant design changes since it was first developed in 1998. This chapter describes the evolution of the design from its original prototype to the device currently being used in field tests at Columbia and Snake river hydropower facilities.

In actual use, the Sensor Fish electronics package is only one part of a "system" necessary to deploy and retrieve sensor fish, download data, and analyze and interpret data. Much of the evolution of the sensor fish design has been the result of unanticipated problems and opportunities that became obvious during its initial deployment.

2.1   Initial Sensor Fish Design: The "Flubber Fish"

Scientists at PNNL developed the original Sensor Fish as an internal initiative. Initial development and proof-of-concept research took place in fiscal years 1998 and 1999. The PNNL's Laboratory Directed Research and Development program provided proof-of-concept funding for the project. The DOE Advanced Hydropower Turbine System (AHTS) program funded field trials.

2.1.1   Design

The goal of the original project was to design and build a functional prototype of a surrogate fish and test the feasibility of the autonomous device for data acquisition.

To be technically feasible, the surrogate fish had to meet the following design specifications (Johnson et al. 1998):

- be small enough to serve as a surrogate for a smolt-size salmonid

- function in an aquatic environment and withstand conditions fish are assumed to experience within a turbine intake

- be capable of storing data for later retrieval.

Size and shape. The size and shape factors for the initial design were obtained by making a plaster cast of a juvenile chinook salmon smolt. Microsensors were placed on a specially designed printed circuit card (Figure 2.1) and covered with a state-of-the-art polymer (Dow Corning 3-4207 Dielectric Tough Gel) designed to give the electronic assembly a fish shape while remaining flexible enough for the forces to activate the internal sensors. A foam layer was imbedded in the tough gel to aid in achieving neutral buoyancy. The overall dimensions of the prototype were approximately 16 cm long and 5.7 cm wide (Figures 2.1 and 2.2). It was nicknamed "flubber fish." Without foam "flubber" had a density of 1.2 gm/cm^3 and a specific gravity of 1.2.

Microsensor transducers to analyze turbine conditions. PNNL researchers defined three types of forces (stress-strain relationships) a fish might experience during turbine passage: tensile force,

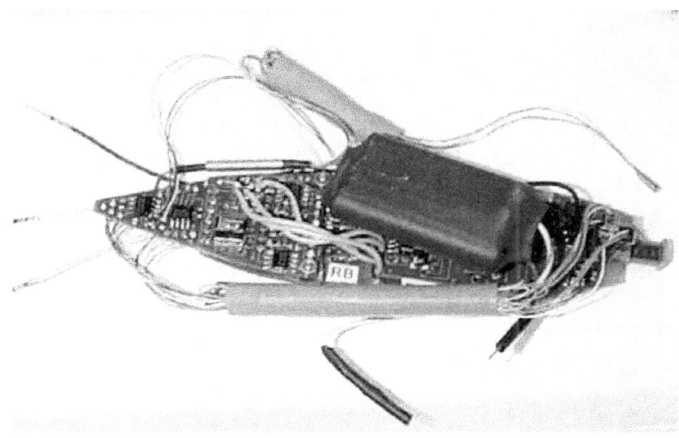

Figure 2.1.   Pressure Transducer, Accelerometer, and Strain Gages in Sensor Fish Device

Figure 2.2.   Initial Sensor Fish Device

compression, and shear strain (Johnson et al. 1998). To measure these forces, researchers selected six strain gages from MicroMeasurement's Division of Measurement Group, Inc. Two strain gages were positioned in the nose area of the fish, one on the right side and one on the left side. Four strain gages were placed in the middle body area of the surrogate fish, two on the right side (top and bottom) and two on the left side (Johnson et al. 1998). The circuit boards were pieced so that shear, tensile, and compression forces would be more accurate.

The sensor fish was equipped with three Entran EGA accelerometers (Figure 2.3) in a tri-axial configuration to measure acceleration using x-, y-, and z-axes. The positive x-axis was in the forward direction of the surrogate fish. The positive y-axis was in the downward direction of the surrogate fish, and the positive z-axis was lateral to the right of the surrogate fish.

An Entran EPI pressure transducer (Figure 2.4) also was placed in the surrogate fish to measure total pressure encountered during turbine passage and to estimate the depth of the sensor within the water column. This transducer was placed in the "nose" region of the sensor fish.

Figure 2.3.   Accelerometer Contained in Prototype Sensor Fish Device

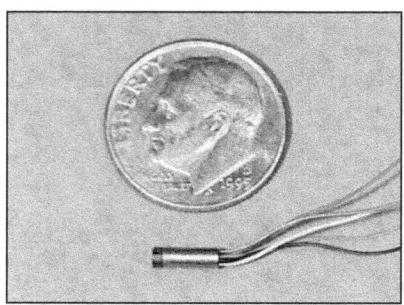

Figure 2.4.   Pressure Transducer Contained in Prototype Sensor Fish Device

Data storage and retrieval. The single responses measured by the 10 transducers within the Sensor Fish were fed into an Analog Devices Precision Single Supply Instrumentation Amplifier, AMPO4. The six strain gages and three accelerometers had a gain of 100 (40 dB), and the pressure transducer had a gain of 50 (34 dB). Each amplified signal then went into an input channel of a Maxim Low-Power, 8-Channel, Serial 12-Bit ADCs MAX 186. The analog signal was then converted into a 12-bit digital signal that was retrieved via Serial Peripheral Interface.

A mid-range 8-bit microcontroller, Microchip PIC16C67, was used as the controller of the Sensor Fish data logger (fdl) system. The PIC16CXX Instruction Set was used to program the controller. When the battery of the fish was connected, a time delay of approximately 1 minute occurred, allowing the battery-backed memory to come on line with the system. The microchip controller then collected and logged data from the 10 sensors at a sampling rate of 40 Hz for approximately 10.9 minutes. Data were stored in a Nonvolatile SRAM chip (4096K) that was backed up with a battery module that snapped on top of the SRAM chip. Data were loaded on the bus to read/write.

Power to the surrogate fish originally was supplied using two 1.5-volt AAA Energizer batteries. These batteries were hooked in a series to give an output of 3.0 volts. However, because the CMOS/TTL needed 5 volts to run, a Maxim MAX756 3.3 V/5V, Step-Up DC-DC Converter was used to provide the necessary 5-volt power supply.

Data download was accomplished using wires embedded in the tail of the Sensor Fish. Wires were exposed and connected to a RS232 port on a computer containing the fish downloading software. A 5-volt power supply, consisting of positive and negative leads, and a power transformer, which plugged into a conventional outlet, were connected to the Sensor Fish, the positive lead to the male battery lead wire and the negative lead to the ground wire in the tail. Following connection, the transducers were checked for functionality, and data downloading was started. Following download, the Sensor Fish was reset so it was ready for data collection.

2.1.2   Laboratory Tests

During development of the first prototype, PNNL scientists conducted a series of laboratory tests to evaluate the performance of various sensors in the Sensor Fish device. In 1998, in controlled laboratory tests, the Sensor Fish was subjected to a range of conditions such as pressure and shear stress that a fish would experience in a turbine environment. Repeat test measurements were recorded to determine how well the surrogate fish measured the forces that acted on it.

Pressure sensor calibration. Experiments were carried out in the laboratory to evaluate the effectiveness of the Sensor Fish pressure transducer. A Rapid Decompression Testing Chamber (hyperbaric chamber), which simulates the rapid pressure changes fish encounter passing through a large turbine, was used to evaluate the transducer (Abernethy et al. 2001). The chamber simulated a rapid pressure change from about 58 psia to less than 1 psia in approximately 0.1 second and recorded data to a computer that controlled the chamber. The Sensor Fish was introduced into the chamber, and the pressure sequence was initiated. Data were downloaded, and the sensor fish data and chamber data were compared. Results were remarkably similar, indicating the pressure sensor, calibration factors, analog to digital converter, and other digital electronics were all performing as expected.

Shear stress. A prototype shear test facility was designed and built at PNNL to perform preliminary tests exposing fish to shear stresses estimated to be as high as ~4,000 Newtons per meter^2 (Neitzel et al. 2000). The system was designed to produce the desired stresses when ~190 liters/minute of water passed through a submerged jet nozzle at a velocity of ~18 m/sec. In a series of approximately 15 tests, the Sensor Fish device was introduced to a jet plume of water for a fraction of a second. The fish was then recovered and repeatedly re-introduced to the shear force until the Sensor Fish's memory was full (Johnson et al. 1998). The results of these tests indicated that, in general, the higher the level of turbulence exposure, the higher the strain measured by the sensor's strain gages.

2.1.3   Field Tests

Field trials of the prototype design were conducted in late May and early June 1999 at McNary Dam on the Columbia River. Flows during the period ranged from approximately 170 to 220 kcfs. Discharge through the test turbine unit was approximately 12 kcfs.

Initial testing in the field environment used non-instrumented fish to assess physical damage caused by turbine passage and determine the retrievability of the sensor fish from the tailrace. Figure 2.5 shows the process used to acquire data with the Sensor Fish. The device is released from the intake (forebay) deck on the forebay side of the dam into the inlet of an induction system consisting of a head tank, pipe, and control valves (Carlson 2000). The pipe extended from the intake deck to the test turbine stay vanes immediately upstream of the turbine runner blades. In preparation for deployment, Hi-Z tags, specially designed balloons containing a gas-producing chemical, were attached to the Sensor Fish, along with a

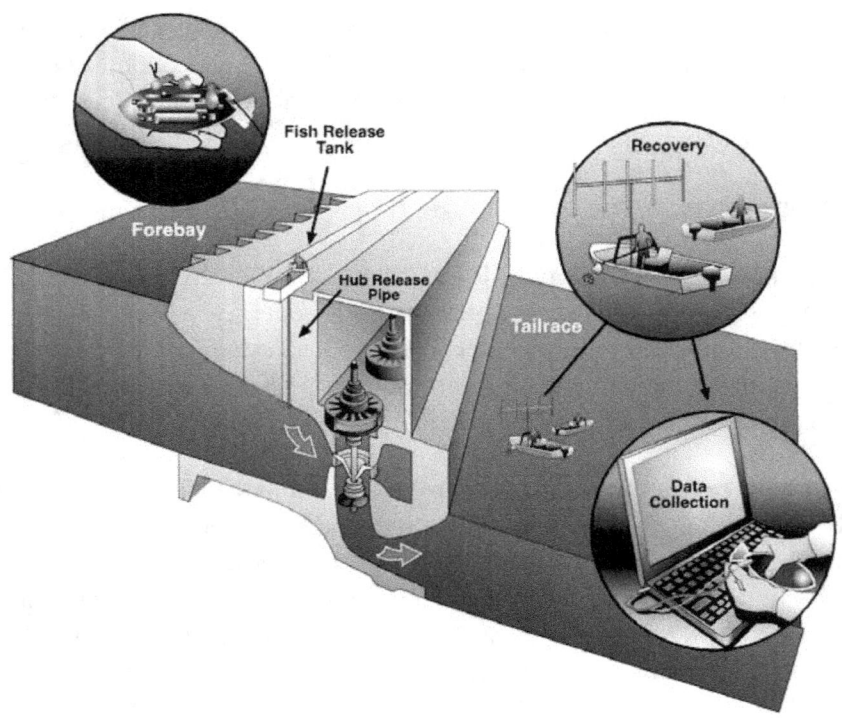

Figure 2.5.   Sensor Fish Data Acquisition Process

micro-radio transmitter. A few seconds before the sensor was released into the induction system, a small amount of hot water is injected into the balloons. The hot water immediately begins to dissolve a capsule surrounding a gas-producing chemical. No gas is produced during the few seconds required for the sensor to pass through the turbine. The balloons inflated within a few minutes of release and brought the non-instrumented fish to the tailrace surface.

Following successful deployment and recovery of "dummy" fish, fully instrumented Sensor Fish were deployed into the test turbine using the induction system.

The first extensive field use of the prototype Sensor Fish device occurred at Bonneville Dam in November 1999 to January 2000 during evaluation of the biological performance of a minimum gap runner (MGR) turbine installed at Bonneville Dam's first powerhouse (Normandeau Associates and Skalski 2001).

2.1.4   Assessment

The original Sensor Fish design failed during initial field trials for several reasons. The most significant were failure of the accelerometers because of low shock (overdrive) protection, difficulty and cost of repair, and difficulties in retrieving the Sensor Fish. Although the fish-shaped potting material was visually appealing, it took considerable time to remove the potting from the electronic components so they could be repaired. In addition, some Sensor Fish were lost because of a combination of factors: Cold water temperatures decreased the rate and yield of gas production in the recovery balloons, the initial Sensor Fish had high negative buoyancy (specific gravity 1.2), and hydrostatic pressure greater that two atmospheres caused the recovery method to fail. Also, if the rubber cover was cut during testing, the foam layer for buoyancy acted like a sponge, further decreasing Sensor Fish buoyancy.

2.1.5   Design Modifications

The development of the original prototype underwent some modifications as a result of physical and experimental requirements. For example, the battery package used to power the microprocessor and sensors was converted from two AAA batteries to a series of three AAAA rechargeable batteries. This resulted in a size reduction in the width of the surrogate, making it more analogous to that of an actual smolt.

The foam layer imbedded in the tough gel surrounding the Sensor Fish was eliminated following problems with water leakage, which corrupted or destroyed data. Conformal coatings and shrink-wrapping were evaluated in an attempt to prevent water leakage.

In October 1999, the sampling rate of the microchip controller was adjusted to 400 Hz. This provided more data points for analysis, while shifting the data log time to approximately 1 minute. The time-delay before logging began was adjusted to 1.5 minutes. Following analyses of the 400-Hz data, it was determined that a 200-hz setting, providing a 2-minute data log time would be optimal. The time-delay before data acquisition was initiated was modified to 1 minute.

In December 1999, LED readout was added to the prototype to enable the operator to determine the state of the sensor, particularly the onset of data acquisition. The LED was designed to flash three times following the 1-minute delay time. This enabled the operator to determine when data collection began. In the event the LED did not flash, the operator recognized that a problem existed, and the sensor should not be deployed. A constant LED readout indicated the battery power was depleted, or the Sensor Fish was not reset. Following download and resetting of the Sensor Fish, the LED would flash three times, indicating the device was ready to collect data.

2.2   Redesigned Sensor Fish Device: PVC Pipe

The second iteration of the design relied on a PVC tube housing with screw-in end caps (Figure 2.6) This "pipe-configuration" surrogate fish was developed to promote data downloading and access to electronics. This redesign had to be accomplished in a few days to avoid losing sampling time during the ongoing minimum gap runner (MGR) biological test at Bonneville Dam. Therefore, materials readily available from local hardware shops and quickly available from other vendors were used.

2.2.1   Design

The original design was of PVC pipe with the batteries protruding from one end and the download leads and pressure transducer protruding from the opposite end. Wire was wrapped around the exterior length of the pipe for weight to make the sensor package neutrally buoyant. The sensors used in the design were pressure gages and x-, y-, and z-accelerometers.

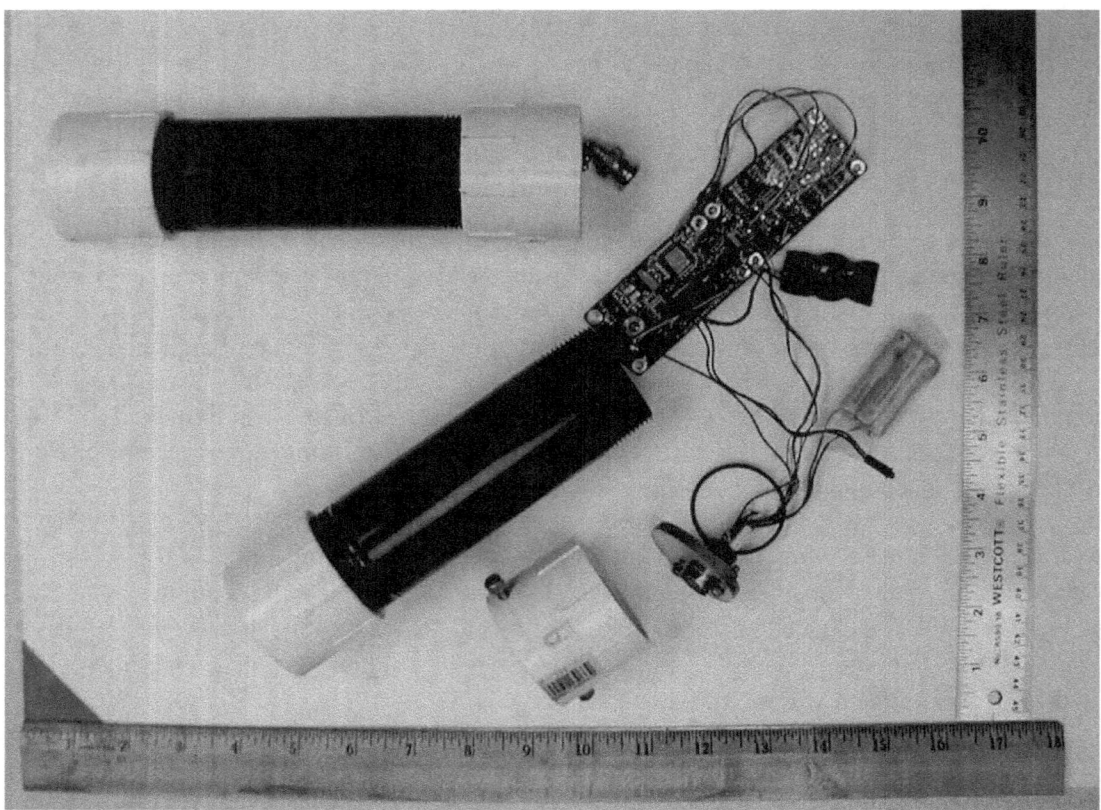

Figure 2.6.   Redesigned Sensor Fish Device: PVC Pipe

2.2.2   Laboratory Tests

No laboratory tests were conducted with this Sensor Fish device. The same circuitry and pressure and acceleration transducers used in the original sensor fish were simply repackaged.

2.2.3   Field Tests

The new sensor package was deployed at Bonneville Dam on the Columbia River in December 1999-January 2000 to continue the biological evaluation of the MGR turbine (Normandeau Associates 2000; Carlson 2001). Tests were conducted at four turbine discharge flows: low, medium-low, medium-high, and high, and through the turbine at the hub, center, and tip positions of the blade. Both the new MGR turbine (at Unit 6) and existing turbine (Unit 5) were assessed.

2.2.4   Design Modifications

Field testing of the first PVC prototype units demonstrated that leakage occurred through the threads of the endcaps, shorting the sensors. In early January 2000, O-rings were added to seal the endcaps. The battery wires were replaced with a twist-on through hole connector that powered the batteries when coupled. On the opposite end of the pipe, the download wires were replaced with another through-hole connector that served to download the data and recharge the batteries. This was sealed under a watertight cap that was held in place with four screws. With these modifications, the sensor could be sealed and used without having to break the seal to recharge batteries or download data.

To obtain neutral buoyancy, rigid plastic tubing was wrapped around the unit. This representation of the sensor fish was adequate for use in the Bonneville Dam turbine testing, but some units cracked and subsequently leaked when striking the turbine blade or other turbine structures, so further redesign was warranted.

In addition, during these field tests, the need for shock protection on the accelerometers became very apparent. Over the course of the study, all the accelerometers in all the PVC Sensor Fish devices were irreparably damaged. The net result was that while a great deal of pressure history information was acquired during the study, very few acceleration data were acquired.

2.3   Redesigned Sensor Fish II: Polycarbonate Tube

In May 2000, following the Bonneville MGR test, PNNL scientists designed and built a new cylindrical sensor fish package using polycarbonate plastic (Figure 2.7). The electronics within the unit were coated with RTV (a waterproof coating for electronic components) for waterproofing in the event of O-ring failure.

2.3.1   Design

The redesigned sensor housing is constructed of clear polycarbonate plastic. The device is 7.4 in. long (~188 mm) and 2 in. (~51 mm) in diameter. In addition to the new packaging, the printed circuit cards for the sensor were redesigned to make manufacture and repair easier and less costly. Features were added to simplify use and provide feedback to the user about the Sensor Fish's status (i.e., standby, data acquisition, mode, etc.). The strain sensors were removed because of inconclusiveness in the data obtained and because the new packaging was not conducive for their use. The new design is also nearly neutrally buoyant in fresh water at a temperature of 14°C. Most importantly, a new accelerometer with shock protection (5,000 g overload rating) was specified and built into the polycarbonate sensor.

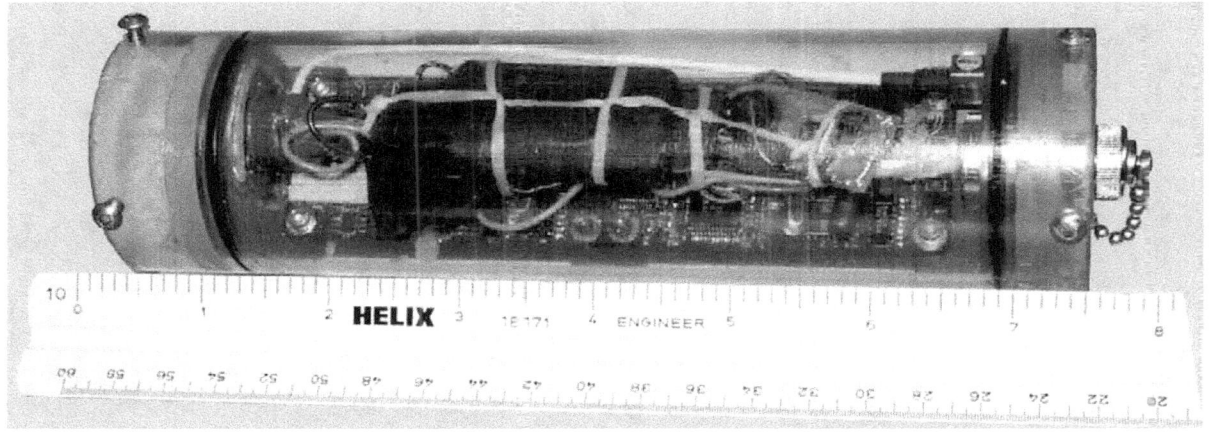

Figure 2.7.   Redesigned Sensor Fish II: Polycarbonate Plastic Tube

2.3.2   Laboratory Tests

The new sensor package was evaluated in the hyperbaric chamber. As in the case of the original Sensor Fish, acquired pressure data closely mimicked that measured by the hyperbaric chamber pressure controller. Laboratory testing also included static and dynamic testing of accelerometers. Results of these tests showed that the accelerometers were performing as expected.

2.3.3   Field Tests

Since summer 2000, the polycarbonate Sensor Fish has been successfully used in a number of projects to characterize passage conditions through turbines, spillways, and sluiceways. These include field studies at Rock Island, McNary, The Dalles, and Bonneville dams. See Section 4.0 for examples of results from these studies (Carlson and Duncan 2002a and 2002b).

2.3.4   Assessment

Although the polycarbonate Sensor Fish was successful, there were plenty of opportunities for improvement. The device was larger than desirable and did not mimic the size and shape of juvenile smolt. It was expensive to manufacture and repair; used proprietary software; required too much time to download data (1.3 hours); consumed too much power; required long battery recharge time (4 to 5 hours); and had too little data memory, problems moving through some types of test fish injection systems, and complicated procedures for activation, battery coupling, and data download.

3.0   Sensor Fish Data Acquisition and Analysis

3.1   Data Acquisition

The first step in acquisition of data with a Sensor Fish is placing (or injecting) it into the flow field at a location of interest. All Sensor Fish studies have been conducted concurrently with live fish studies and have used the same injection systems used to place live test fish within a turbine or spill flow field at an operating hydroelectric dam. These injection systems consist of various configurations of hoses, pumps. and holding tanks that permit safe handling of live fish and also provide the water necessary to move test fish from the surface into a flow field.

Researchers standing on the deck of the dam drop the fish or Sensor Fish into the inlet of a water-filled pipe, which carries the fish to the desired release location in the flow field of a turbine intake or in a spill discharge jet (Figure 3.1). Simple injection systems use water flowing under the force of gravity to transport the fish into the flow field. More complex injection systems used for turbine passage route-specific studies of fish survival include a head tank and are designed so that the exit velocity of the fish and water closely match that of the ambient flow at the point of injection (Carlson 2000). This type of injection system, while providing the control of release location and conditions needed for some studies, requires specialized engineering and installation methods and is costly.

Figure 3.1.   Injection System Used to Deploy Sensor Fish

The HiZ Turb-N-Tag method, developed by Normandeau Associates, is used to tag the sensor fish, deploy it into a test environment (e.g., spillway or turbine), and recover it following dam passage. In this method, specialized balloons containing a capsule filled with a chemical are attached to a fish. A micro-radio transmitter is also attached to the fish. Approximately 90 seconds before injection the countdown timer in the Sensor Fish is activated, and the micro-radio transmitter is turned on and checked for operation. This is followed, approximately 10 seconds prior to induction, by injection of a small amount of hot water into the balloons attached to the Sensor Fish. When the indicator light activates, alerting the operator that data acquisition has begun, the Sensor Fish is placed in the induction system. The polycarbonate Sensor Fish currently in use has the capacity of 120 seconds of data acquisition from a pressure transducer and three accelerometers at a digital rate of 200 samples per second per sensor. The Sensor Fish's fact-finding journey through the dam typically takes less than 30 seconds for a turbine and 120 seconds for a spill bay.

The warm water injected into the balloons dissolves a capsule filled with a gas-producing chemical within the balloon and a chemical reaction begins within 2 to 5 minutes. The chemical reaction produces enough gas to inflate the balloons, bringing the live test fish (or Sensor Fish) to the surface in the tailrace below the dam. Production of gas in the balloons is delayed by the time required for the capsule enclosing the chemicals that react with water to dissolve to produce carbon dioxide. This time delay can be manipulated to some extent by the temperature of the water injected into the balloons. Once the Sensor Fish has passed through the dam and been brought to the surface by the balloons, a crew working from a boat in the tailrace recovers the fish. The location of the fish is aided by the use of directive radio receivers on the recovery boat. The balloon tag recovery method works well if the Sensor Fish is nearly neutrally buoyant.

The equipment, time, and skill required for successful injection of a Sensor Fish into a complex hydraulic environment and subsequent recovery is considerable. Because of the setup costs involved, field use of the Sensor Fish has often been timed to coincide with live fish studies when live fish are also being radio- and balloon-tagged and sent through the dams. One fortunate result is that most Sensor Fish data sets collected so far can be paired with live fish data, including survival rates and observations of injury type collected under the same river flow and turbine conditions.

3.2 Data Analysis

The primary data obtained with the polycarbonate Sensor Fish currently being used consists of five columns of numbers: the sample time in increments of 0.005 seconds relative to time zero, total pressure in pounds per square inch, and three columns of acceleration values in gs corresponding to the x-, y-, and z-tri axial coordinates.

The pressure output is converted to gage pressure by subtracting the atmospheric pressure measured when the sensor was exposed to air before injection. The pressure output is useful in indicating the depth of the sensor at specific times. Features of the pressure time history are also very helpful in estimating the location of the sensor at particular times. The accelerometer output is typically processed by converting g to ft/sec^2 and computing the components of the resultant acceleration vector, jerk, or other quantity of interest. Examples of typical output and their interpretation are shown in the examples in the following section.

4.0   Case Studies

A growing number of hydroelectric dam operators in the Northwest have recognized the value of the Sensor Fish device as a way to collect data that help us better understand the injury mechanisms specific to their facility. During the last few years, PNNL researchers have deployed the Sensor Fish device at Rock Island, McNary, The Dalles, Bonneville, and Wanapum dams on the Columbia River and the Prosser Irrigation District on the Yakima River. The device helps identify injury mechanisms for fish such as strike and shear, and inertial effects, including indirect effects like stunning and other signs of vestibular disruption.

Three deployments are presented here that represent the broad application of the Sensor Fish device. They include a turbine environment at McNary Dam tested in summer 2002, a spillway environment at The Dalles Dam tested in summer 2000, and a high-volume free-fall spill at Rock Island Dam tested in November 2001.

4.1   Passage through a Turbine

Most injuries to fish appear to occur in the runner region of a dam's turbine (Čada et al. 1997; Monten 1985; Turnpenny 1998; McEwen and Scobie 1992). Figure 4.1 shows a visualization of the approach of the flow to the runner, water movement along the runner, and direction of flow immediately below the runner of a Kaplan turbine.

At McNary Dam, most injuries to fish passing through the turbine appear to take place in close proximity to the blades. Little information existed on what inertial effects fish experience near the turbine blades. To examine this issue, the U.S. Army Corps of Engineers, Walla Walla District, asked PNNL to conduct Sensor Fish studies at McNary Dam.

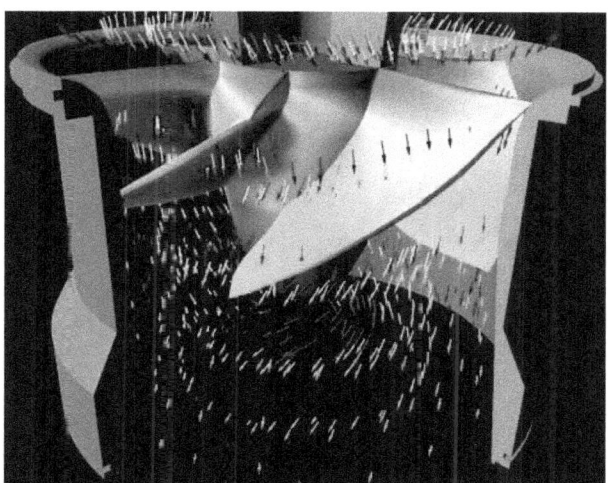

Figure 4.1.   **Turbine Flow Visualization. Visualization by ETH Zurich (R. Peikert, M. Roth), CFD Simulation by Escher Wyss, Zurich, Switzerland**

We conducted 50 test releases through the Kaplan turbine at Unit 9. Sensor Fish were released at two discharges and all three intake bays upstream of the scroll case in the plane of the emergency gate slot.

One set of data collected by the Sensor Fish shows the typical pressure drop (at about 38.5 seconds) as flow accelerates through the turbine runner (Figure 4.2). The difference in pressure above and below the runner blades is needed to force the turbine runner to rotate.

The acceleration magnitudes corresponding to this pressure time history are shown in Figure 4.3. These data indicate the greatest changes in velocity occurred as the Sensor Fish passed the turbine runner and again at the backroll upon exit from the draft tube (at approximately 44 seconds).

Because the Sensor Fish simultaneously samples pressure and acceleration, the time interval is the same for pressure and acceleration data. The acceleration magnitude maximum seen in Figure 4.3 corresponds to the pressure minimum shown in Figure 4.2 and occurs as the Sensor Fish drops through the runner. This unique feature in the pressure time history greatly aids identification of the location of the sensor at a particular time during turbine transit. This is expected because the pressure in the fluid should be lowest when the velocity of water is highest. The "bumps" in acceleration on the left side of the peak as the sensor approaches the runner can be seen clearly in Figure 4.3. The time interval between these peaks is approximately 0.145 seconds, which is roughly the period between passage of turbine blades past a point on the discharge ring. It appears that the flow through the runner is modulated by interplay between the movement of runner blades and the wicket gate openings. The result is the "pulsing" in the movement of the Sensor Fish as it is carried by the water.

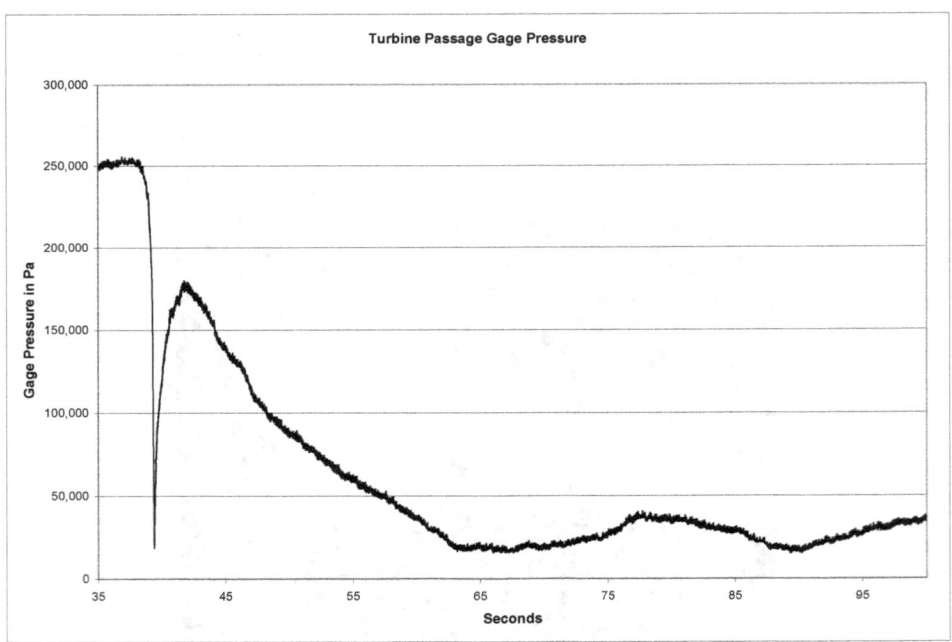

Figure 4.2. **Pressure Data for Sensor Fish Passing through Turbine Unit 9 at McNary Dam Showing Pressure Drop as Sensor Fish Drops through Turbine**

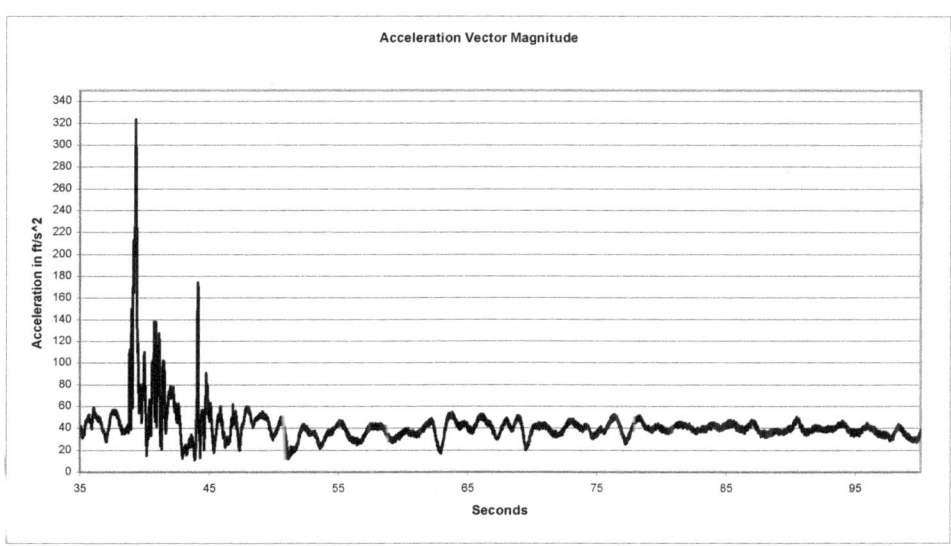

Figure 4.3.   Acceleration Data for Sensor Fish Passing through Turbine Unit 9 at McNary Dam

This result demonstrates the detail about hydraulic conditions immediately above a turbine runner that can be observed using the Sensor Fish. In particular, it is clear that the acceleration of the water approaching the runner is not smooth, but rather, a "surging" flow with a number of distinctive acceleration and deceleration cycles of relatively high magnitude.

There is considerable variability in acceleration time histories that appears to be related to the location of the sensor as it passes through the turbine wicket gates and differences in its trajectory during approach to the runner. Also, it is worth noting that this "surging" action is propagated downstream of the draft tube exit into the powerhouse tailrace.

One hypothesis, based on data from the Sensor Fish study and evidence of shear-like injuries seen in live fish with the McNary turbine study, is that some of the fish's injuries may result from inertial effects where fish are accelerated at a lower rate than the surrounding fluid. This suggests that smaller fish (e.g., subyearling chinook salmon) are less likely to experience physical injuries because they have less inertia. Laboratory studies show they are also more likely to experience vestibular disruption in the form of disorientation (Neitzel et al. 2000), which can lead to higher indirect mortality from predation. Yet larger fish (e.g., age 1 smolts), with greater inertia, are more likely to experience shear-type injuries such as torn opercula and gill and eye injuries.

4.2   Passage through Spill

Efforts are underway to optimize the use of spill for fish passage. However, it appears likely that some spill conditions are hazardous to fish. Of particular concern are conditions of very high-energy dissipation accompanied by formation of backrollers and reentrainment of lateral flows in stilling basins and other basins receiving bypass outfalls. In the case of spill, high-energy dissipation conditions are known to occur over a range of discharge-tailwater combinations during voluntary and involuntary spill and, for some basins there is significant reentrainment of lateral flows, which greatly extends the time of exposure to very high turbulence conditions. What is not clear is the contribution of direct and indirect effects to fish mortality during dam bypass through spill and the mechanisms of nonlethal injury during exposure to severe hydraulic events that are factors in indirect mortality.

In response to this issue, we conducted studies at The Dalles Dam in May and August 2000 using the Sensor Fish device. The purpose of the studies was to describe the time-varying and location-specific conditions fish experience during passage through spill environments. Six tailwater-discharge pairs were identified for sampling. At each tailwater-discharge pair a total of 20 Sensor Fish devices were released to measure pressure and tri-axial acceleration.

Table 4.1 summarizes estimates of stilling basin retention time for Sensor Fish and an index of the intensity of exposure to turbulent stilling basin conditions. Although the number of releases per spillbay was nearly the same, the releases were not equally distributed over the various gate openings for each spillbay. In addition, the only discharge common to all spillbays was 6.00 kcfs. This was the minimum discharge for spillbay 4 and the maximum discharge for spillbay 13.

Stilling basin retention time was estimated using Sensor Fish pressure time histories. These time histories indicate the depth of the sensor as a function of time following release of the Sensor Fish into the spill environment at the tainter gate. Stilling basin exit was taken to be that time when the sensor stopped depth cycling, (which indicates involvement in large-scale turbulent eddies within the stilling basin) and moved up in the water column and remained at shallow depth. Refinement in these estimates will be possible when CFD-based estimates of particle retention times are available.

The intensity of exposure to turbulent stilling basin conditions was estimated by summing the magnitude of the acceleration vector computed using the time history of accelerations measured on each axis of the Sensor Fish's tri-axial accelerometer cluster. This would be proportional to the area under the curve in Figure 4.3.

The stilling basin retention duration estimates and exposure intensity index are plotted in Figure 4.4. There appears to be a fairly strong relationship between stilling basin retention time and exposure intensity index. This is not surprising since these variables are linked. The exposure index is the acceleration vector magnitude summed over the stilling basin duration. However, what was surprising was that, after we partially decoupled the exposure index from stilling basin duration by imposing a threshold on acceleration vector magnitude values before including them in the index, we found essentially the same relationship. The accelerations observed during passage through the stilling basin dominate the index. The higher exposure index values at lower discharge result from the additional turbulent cycles that the sensor fish experiences when it remains in the stilling basin an additional period of time. The time for a single additional cycles appears to be on the order of approximately 10 sec. An example of a sensor fish gage pressure time history is shown in Figure 4.5.

The range in the exposure intensity index is a factor of two from approximately 4E+5 to 8E+5 ft/sec^2. Once CFD analyses have been done it will be possible to compare these data with estimates of stilling basin energy dissipation density and other factors. The highest exposure indices observed were for 3 kcfs

Table 4.1. **Spilling Basin Retention Times and Intensity of Exposures to Turbulence for Sensor Fish Released in The Dalles Stilling Basin**

Spillbay	Spillbay Discharge (kcfs)	Sample Size (no. of sensor fish releases)	Mean Duration (sec)	Duration Standard Deviation	Mean Acceleration Vector Magnitude Sum (ft/sec^2)	Acceleration Vector Magnitude Sum Standard Deviation
4	6.00	5	49.3	9.0	6.491E+05	1.184E+05
4	7.50	10	59.2	29.5	7.562E+05	4.222E−05
4	9.00	21	52.3	23.9	6.614E+05	3.415E−05
4	10.50	9	38.8	14.1	4.864E+05	1.869E−05
9	4.50	5	56.6	15.8	5.963E+05	2.162E−05
9	6.00	20	45.1	19.7	5.789E+05	2.338E−05
9	7.50	18	48.1	25.3	6.069E+05	4.019E+05
13	3.00	35	60.1	23.0	7.483E+05	3.784E+05
13	5.25	5	33.9	17.4	4.127E+05	1.232E+05
13	6.00	5	36.8	9.1	4.207E+05	8.120E+04

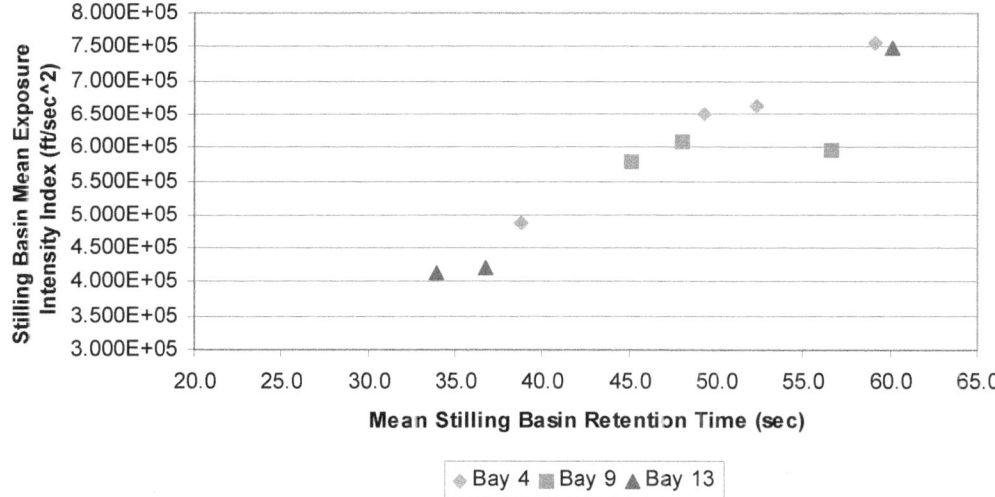

Figure 4.4. **Stilling Basin Mean Exposure Intensity Index for Spillbays by Mean Stilling Basin Retention Time**

discharge at spillbay 13 and 7.5 kcfs discharge at spillbay 4. There doesn't seem to be a large enough increase in turbulence intensity at higher spillbay discharges to offset the increase in the exposure index due to stilling basin retention duration.

Figure 4.6 shows the relationship between spillbay discharge and retention time for this data set. The relationship between stilling basin retention times and spillbay discharge shown is, in general, consistent with the patterns of stilling basin retention times observed using dye in tests with The Dalles Dam

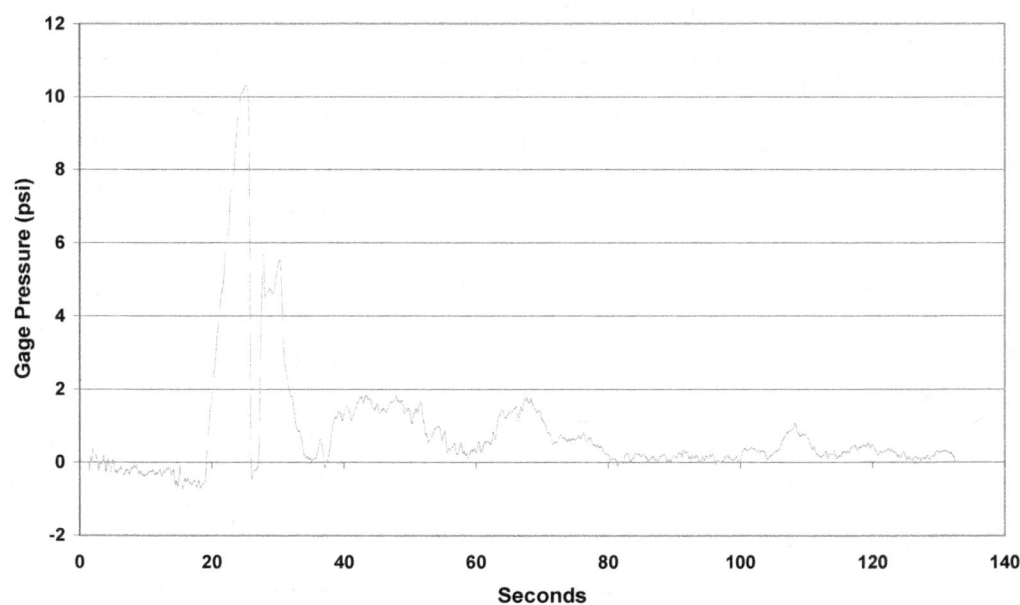

Figure 4.5.   Example of a Sensor Fish Gage Pressure Time History

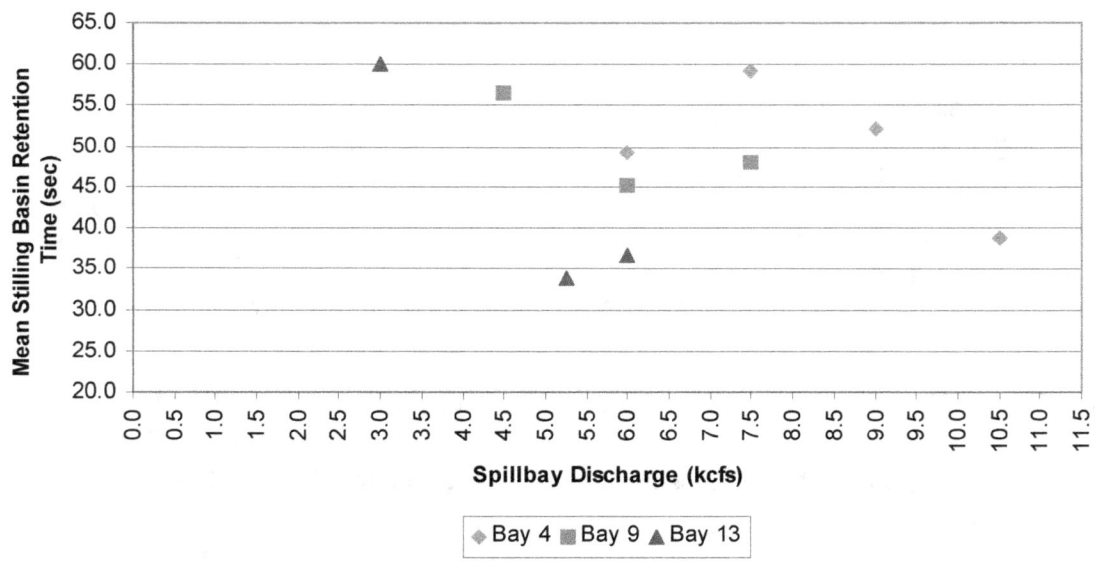

Figure 4.6.   Relationship Between Spillbay Discharge and Exposure Intensity Index

physical model. Figure 4.7 shows a plan view of The Dalles spillbay arrangement. Retention time decreased in the physical model when spillbay discharge was increased at a specific bay. In addition, retention time was higher for the end spillbays at lower discharge because of lateral flow from south to north. Somewhat unexpected were the relatively short stilling basin retention times for spillbay 13 at

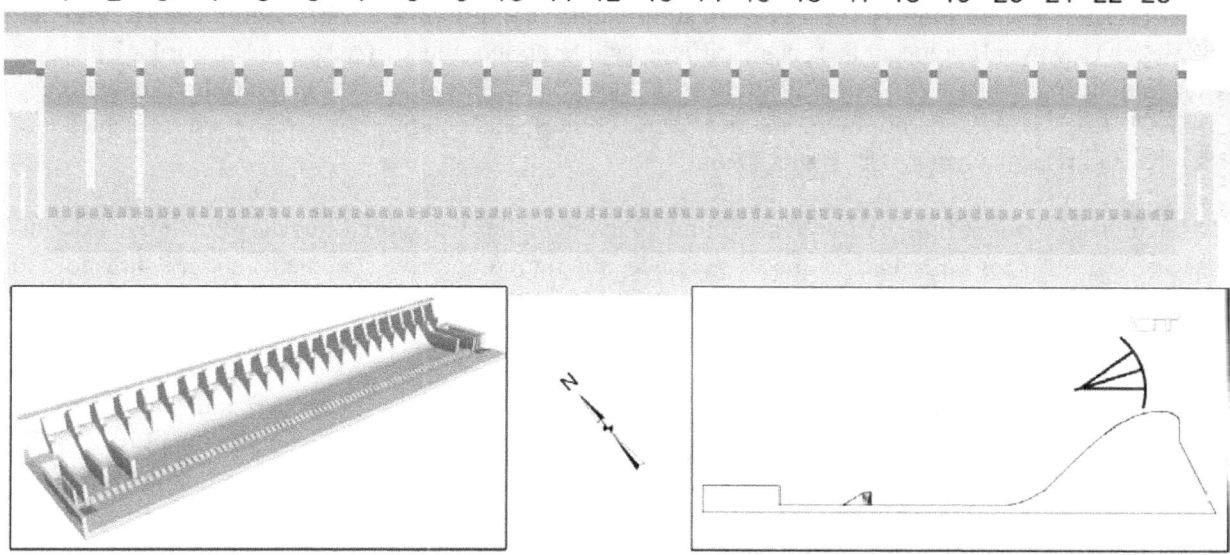

Figure 4.7.   Schematic of The Dalles Dam Spillbay Arrangement

discharges of 5.25 and 6.00 kcfs. The implications of these observations are not clear. For example, are these observations the result of the location of the injection pipe terminus or do the nature of stilling basin dynamics and aspects of lateral flow change with increasing discharge from end bays?

A puzzling question is what these data imply about the relationship between the magnitude of spillbay discharge and direct fish survival. Limited data suggest the direct survival of fish is increased as per bay spill discharge is increased. It also appears that the exposure intensity, as indicated by the index we've computed, decreases with increased spillbay discharge (Table 4.2).

For the range of direct fish survival estimates observed, the percent difference in overall mean exposure intensity index between spillbays 4 and 13 was approximately 4%, while the percent difference in retention time was approximately 7%. The difference in mean fish survival between these two spillbays was approximately 4.5%.

Table 4.2.   Stilling Basin Mean Exposure Intensity Index, Retention Time, and Direct Survival by Spillbay

Spillbay	Stilling Basin Mean Exposure Intensity Index (ft/sec^2)	Still Basin Mean Retention Time (sec)	Mean Fish Direct Survival
Spill Bay 4	6.46E+05	50.81	0.987
Spill Bay 9	6.67E+05	48.98	0.989
Spill Bay 13	6.75E+05	54.61	0.942

In our analysis of sensor fish data to date we have not included any fish injury data or other features of Sensor Fish pressure and acceleration time histories (such as the number, magnitude, and duration of large-scale turbulence eddy cycles experienced by Sensor Fish during stilling basin passage). Additional analysis should provide additional insight into stilling basin conditions and relationships to fish survival and injury. However, it appears that mean stilling basin retention time differences on the order of 5 to 10 sec and mean exposure condition differences on the order of 5% with index magnitudes on the order of 4 to $8E+5$ ft/sec^2 will be the minimum requirements for a test that can be expected to produce detectable differences in fish survival at The Dalles Dam.

A "threshold" for stilling basin retention time to avoid higher fish mortalities may be on the order of 45 sec or less. It is too early in data analysis to make any more definitive statements about a threshold for stilling basin retention time. In addition, it is worth keeping in mind that we have not looked at The Dalles Dam spill in any detail.

The standard deviations associated with estimates of mean duration and exposure index are large, on the order of 50% of mean values. This is consistent with the variability observed in the time histories of Sensor Fish pressure and acceleration. It appears that test spillbay discharge differences on the order of a factor of two will be required to achieve mean exposure condition differences likely to result in detectable, much less statistically significant, direct fish survival differences using sample sizes of 300 or so fish per "treatment." Other conditions may apply for non-lethal injury.

Data analysis so far has not resolved any tradeoff between spillbay discharge rate, exposure intensity, and retention time. It appears that stilling basin duration is less variable than exposure intensity, and that fish direct survival may be more sensitive to mean duration than mean exposure intensity. However, turbulence intensity and retention time are confounded. The relationship between spillbay discharge level and turbulence intensity and/or retention time is a function of stilling basin hydraulics, i.e., the (hydraulic) relationship between bays. It is possible to get very different measures of exposure conditions and fish survival for the same spillbay discharge depending on the stilling basin conditions created by spill pattern. This is not new information, but is now made more obvious, and it helps explain the difficulties experienced in previous studies in detecting linkage between details of spill operation and fish survival.

4.3 High-Volume Free-Fall Spill

At Rock Island Dam, the Chelan County Public Utility District (PUD) has modified a spillbay by installing a bulkhead with an adjustable slot across the spillbay gate opening (Figure 4.8). The intent of this modification was to attract surface-oriented juvenile salmon to pass in spill rather than through turbines. The PUD also installed a deflector in the spill stilling basin to help control dissolved gas concentrations in the spill plume. The deflector was submerged approximately 4 ft.

We evaluated the potential impacts of this spill configuration on salmonid survival in November 2000 and December 2001 using live fish and the Sensor Fish device (Normandeau Associates and Skalski 2001; Carlson and Duncan 2002a).

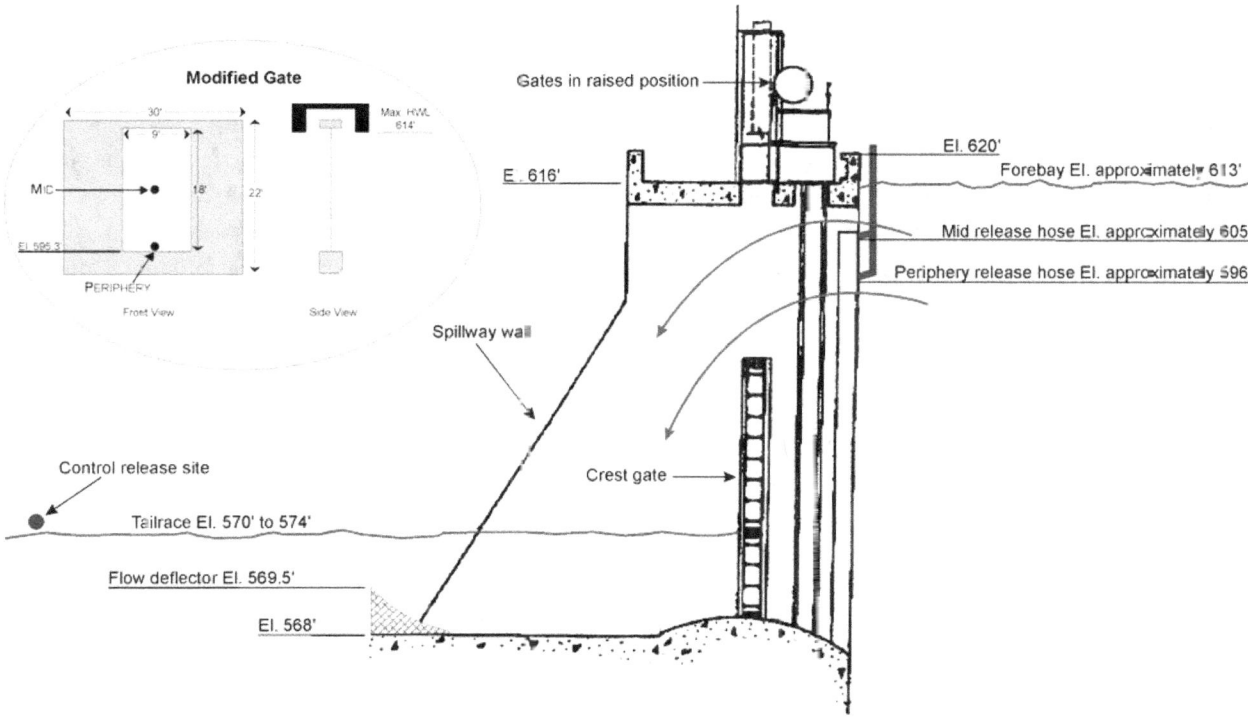

Figure 4.8.   Cross-Section of the Rock Island Dam Spillway Showing the Release Hose Positions and the Notched Spill Gate

A total of 31 Sensor Fish were released into a spill discharge of 2.5 kcfs from two locations immediately upstream of the spill opening: 14 were released at a mid-spill discharge release midway in the gate opening (at elevation 605 ft above mean sea level), 14 were released at a periphery release near the lower edge of the 18-ft-high gate opening, and 3 were released directly into the spill discharge downstream of the deflector in a "reference" release for comparison.

The forebay and tailwater elevations were near 613 and 571 ft, respectively, at the time of the test so fish passed in top spill experienced a free fall of approximately 45 ft onto the shallowly submerged spill deflector in the stilling basin. The depth of water at the bottom of the stilling basin was 4 ft, dropping to 30 to 40 ft downstream of the flow deflector. Nearly every Sensor Fish released into spill discharge appeared to strike the bottom of the stilling basin or the deflector. The duration of the strike impulse of the Sensor Fish was typically ~85 m/sec with peak acceleration vector magnitudes within the range of 15 to 30 g.

Following the strike impulse, the Sensor Fish were carried downstream, which indicated that the deflector may not have performed well. It appears that the lower edge of the spill discharge jet supports the upper portion of the jet. For spill periphery-released Sensor Fish, 11 of 13 were carried to depths of at least 2.3 ft, while 7 of 13 were carried to depths of at least 4.6 ft. The maximum depth recorded for any peripheral release was approximately 12.5 ft.

Sensor Fish released in the middle of the spill discharge tended to be less likely to be carried to depth. Only 9 of 13 mid-spill releases resulted in the Sensor Fish being carried to depths greater than 2.3 ft, and only 4 of the 13 were carried to depths greater than 4.6 ft. One of the mid-spill-released Sensor Fish was carried to a depth of at least 16 ft, approximately 80 sec after entry into the spill discharge. Both Sensor Fish reference releases were carried to depths of at least 7 ft (~3 psi gage); one was carried to a maximum depth of approximately 12 ft (~5.2 psi gage). It is clear that the dynamics of the spill discharge jet are complex, especially downstream of the stilling basin. Depth cycling of this nature is not believed to negatively impact migrating fish but can, in the case of a well-aerated spill discharge jet, increase total dissolved gas concentrations, which can lead to gas bubble trauma in fish. In this case, the depth excursions for the major portion of the jet appeared to be minor.

Using a mathematical index originally created to estimate the probability of head injury to automobile occupants during crashes, we computed the chance that the Sensor Fish deployed at Rock Island Dam experienced strike based on the impact time.

A low rate of direct visible injuries to live balloon-tagged fish was observed during the fish injury study conducted concurrently with the Sensor Fish device study. Even if all the observed injuries to live fish could be attributed to impact, the rates of injury (and coincident risk of injury) would be low. From the results of the balloon-tag and Sensor Fish components of the Rock Island deflector study, it would appear there was a low rate of direct visible injury by strike. In fact, if the conclusions of the investigators conducting the balloon-tag study about the probable mechanism of injury for injured fish are correct, none of the observed injuries were caused by impact (Normandeau Associates and Skalski 2002).

Inertial effects on fish contained in rapidly accelerating flow have been observed to result in differential flow along the body of the fish, which can result in opercular (gill cover) and other injuries, as seen in shear effects tests conducted by PNNL (Neitzel et al. 2000) in a laboratory setting. A change of 2.4 ft/sec in water velocity magnitude over the 0.005-second digital sampling interval of the Sensor Fish corresponds to the Lowest Observed Effect Level (i.e., injury) for juvenile chinook salmon in PNNL shear effects tests for fish entrained in a discharge jet. It was uncommon for this threshold to be exceeded and, when exceeded, the frequency of occurrence of values above the threshold was on the order of 0.1%. This low rate of exceedance indicates the very low probability of a fish experiencing forces that could result in injury as they passed the dam in spill discharge.

The elements of exposure of fish to potentially injurious events during passage through 2.5 kcfs of spill at Rock Island Dam, as measured by the Sensor Fish, indicated low risk of injury by impact on the deflector and low risk of exposure to inertial effects. These observations agree with the low mortality (~1%) and injury rates (~1.5%) for live fish observed during balloon-tag tests conducted at Rock Island Dam concurrently with the Sensor Fish releases (Normandeau Associates and Skalski 2002).

Gage pressure (depth surrogate) and acceleration vector magnitude cumulative distributions for all peripheral releases combined were computed. Figure 4.9 shows the gage pressure cumulative distributions. Acceleration vector magnitude cumulative distributions are shown in Figure 4.10.

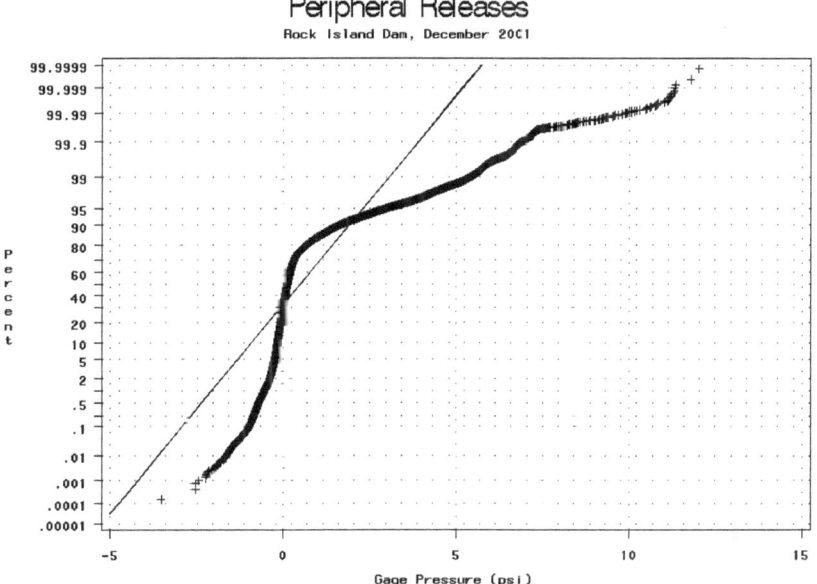

Figure 4.9. **Cumulative Distribution of Gage Pressure for all Peripheral Sensor Fish Releases (+ represents individual pressure readings taken every 0.005 seconds)**

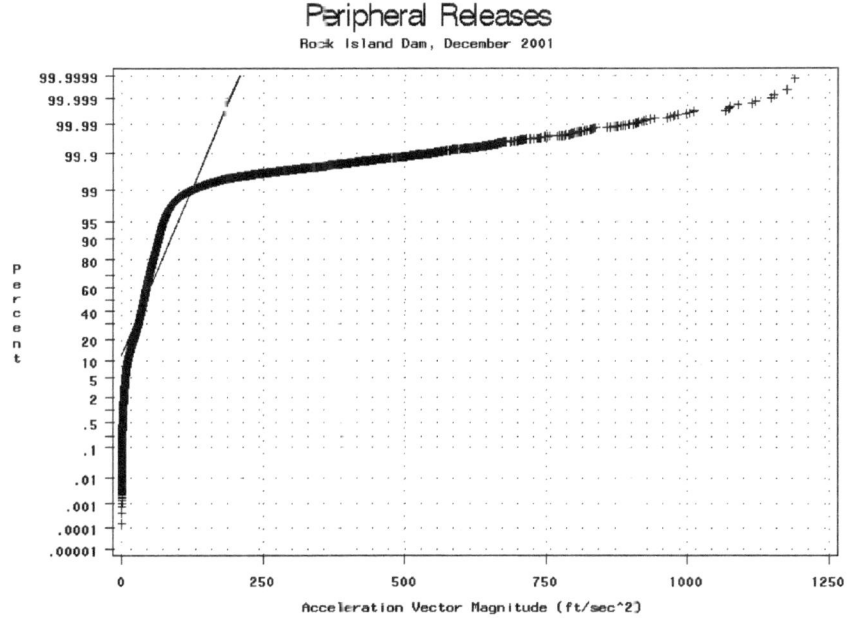

Figure 4.10. Cumulative Distribution of Acceleration Vector Magnitude for all Peripheral Sensor Fish Releases

The most surprising overall results of this spill test, given the low submergence of the spill deflector, were the low rate of injury to live test fish (~1.5%) and that few of the injured fish exhibited injury types that could be classified as resulting from impact.

5.0 What's Next

Although the original Sensor Fish design has proven useful in linking passage configurations to fish injury, we have already begun looking forward to the next generation technology. Thanks to advances in electronics component development, significant size reductions are now possible in the Sensor Fish design. A new design effort begun in November 2001 is expected to yield models one-fifth the size and one-fourth the cost to manufacture as the tube-shaped Sensor Fish. The new Sensor Fish models will require less time for data downloading, consume less power, recharge batteries more quickly, store more data, and use nonproprietary software.

Reducing the size of the electronics will allow us to create a Sensor Fish device that can be gastrically inserted into a live smolt. Because it will be a part of the fish, the new Sensor Fish could permit the most realistic view yet of the physical conditions fish are exposed to during dam passage. It could directly link environmental impacts encountered by an individual fish with its injuries. The first prototype insert is approximately 20 mm in diameter and 100 mm in length, which will limit it to be used as a gastric or surgical implant in larger smolt (Figure 5.1). However, an even smaller gastric insert device is being developed that would allow it to be used on smaller smolts. Both prototypes will be ready for testing by early 2003.

Future improvements in the Sensor Fish design could include the addition of rate gyros, which in a larger device could record inertial navigation data and more accurately account for gravitational acceleration.

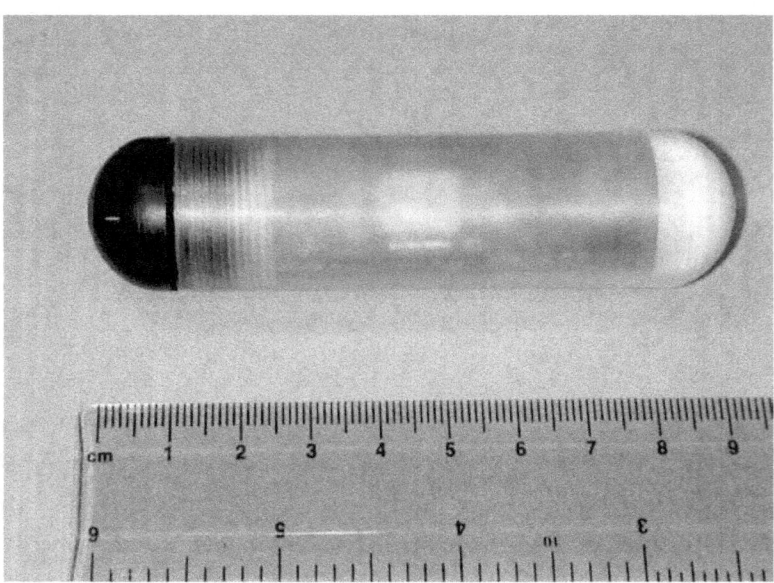

Figure 5.1.   New and Improved Sensor Fish Device

Observations made using the Sensor Fish device already have provided considerable insight into the time history of physical conditions that fish experience during passage through turbines, sluiceways, and in spill. The coupling of Sensor Fish releases with releases of live test fish has permitted correlation of exposure time histories with live fish injury and mortality observations. Measures of duration of exposure to high energy hydraulic events and computation of indices of these exposures that can be used to quantitatively compare structural and operational alternatives will shorten the time and cost required to identify the best passage conditions for fish past dams. Future development of an internalized package of sensors promises closer coupling between the exposures a fish experiences and the consequences of that exposure. This direct linkage between exposure and consequence will further aid the process of finding optimum fish passage solutions.

6.0   References

Abernethy, C. S., B. G. Amidan, and G. F. Čada. 2001. *Laboratory Studies of the Effects of Pressure and Dissolved Gas Supersaturation on Turbine-Passed Fish.* PNNL-13470, Pacific Northwest National Laboratory, Richland, Washington.

Abernethy, C. S., B.G. Amidan, and G. F. Čada. 2002. *Simulated Passage Through a Modified Kaplan Turbine Pressure Regime: A Supplement to "Laboratory Studies of the Effects of Pressure and Dissolved Gas Supersaturation on Turbine-Passed Fish."* PNNL-13470-A, Pacific Northwest National Laboratory, Richland, Washington.

Bell, M. C., and A. C. DeLacy. 1972. *A Compendium on the Survival of Fish Passing Through Spillways and Conduits.* Report to the U.S. Army Corps of Engineers, North Pacific Division, Portland, Oregon.

Bell, M. C. 1981. *Updated Compendium on the Success of Passage of Small Fish Through Turbines.* Report to the U.S. Army Corps of Engineers, North Pacific Division, Portland, Oregon.

Čada, G. F., C .C. Coutant, and R. R. Whitney. 1997. *Development of Biological Criteria for the Design of Advanced Hydroturbines.* U.S. Department of Energy, Idaho Operations Office, DOE/ID-10578, Idaho Falls, Idaho.

Carlson, T. J. (ed.) 2000. *Proceedings of the Turbine Passage Survival Workshop.* Prepared for the U.S. Army Corps of Engineers, Portland District, Portland, Oregon.

Carlson, T. J. 2001. *Sensor Fish Investigation of Fish Passage Through MGR and Existing Units at Bonneville Dam First Powerhouse.* In: Proceedings of the Turbine Passage Survival Workshop, June 14-15, 2000. T. J. Carlson (ed.). Report prepared for the U.S. Army Corps of Engineers, Portland District, Portland, Oregon.

Carlson, T. J., and J. P. Duncan. 2002a. *Characterization of the Hydraulic Environment Experienced by Fish During Passage in Spill at Rock Island Dam, 2001.* PNWD-3156, Battelle, Pacific Northwest Division, Richland, Washington.

Carlson, T. J., and J. P. Duncan. 2002b. *Characterization of the Wanapum Dam Top-Spill Fish Passage Environment.* PNWD-3213, Battelle, Pacific Northwest Division, Richland, Washington.

Johnson, R. L., B. G. Gray, S. L. Blanton, J. P. Duncan, R. W. Gilbert, G. A. Anderson, and D. A. Neitzel. 1998. *Advanced Sensor Tag for Improved Turbine Design.* Pacific Northwest National Laboratory, Internal Report, Richland Washington.

McEwen, D., and G. Scobie. 1992. *Estimation of the Hydraulic Conditions Relating to Fish Passage Through Turbines.* National Engineering Laboratory, East Kilbride, Glasgow, Scotland.

Monten, E. 1985. *Fish and Turbines.* Vattenfall, Stockholm, Sweden, 111 pp.

Neitzel, D. A., M. C. Richmond, D. D. Dauble, R. P. Mueller, R. A. Moursund, C. S. Abernethy, G. R. Guensch, and G. F. Čada. 2000. *Laboratory Studies of the Effects of Shear on Fish*. Prepared for the Advanced Hydropower Turbine System Team, U.S. Department of Energy, Idaho Falls, Idaho, by Pacific Northwest National Laboratory, Richland, Washington.

Normandeau Associates. 2000. *Direct Survival and Condition of Juvenile Chinook Salmon Passed Through an Existing and New Minimum Gap Runner Turbines at Bonneville Dam First Powerhouse, Columbia River*. Report prepared for the U.S. Army Corps of Engineers, Portland District, Portland, Oregon.

Normandeau Associates, Inc., and J. R. Skalski. 2001. *Juvenile Chinook Salmon Survival and Condition After Passage Through a Slotted Spillbay with a Submerged Spill Pool Flow Deflector at Rock Island Dam, Columbia River, Washington*. Report prepared for Public Utility District No. 1 of Chelan County, Wenatchee, Washington.

Normandeau Associates, Inc., and J. R. Skalski. 2002. *Juvenile Chinook Salmon Survival and Condition After Passage Through a Slotted Spillbay with a Shallow Flow Deflector at Rock Island Dam, Columbia River*. Report prepared for Public Utility District No. 1 of Chelan County, Wenatchee, Washington.

Pavlov, D. S., A. I. Lupandin, and V. V. Kostin. 1999. *Downstream Migration of Fish Through Dams of Hydroelectric Power Plants*. Russian Academy of Science, Moscow, Russia.

Ruggles, C. P., and D. G. Murray. 1983. *A Review of Fish Response to Spillways*. Canadian Technical Report of Fisheries and Aquatic Sciences No. 1172.

R2 Resource Consultants, Inc. 1998. *Annotated Bibliography of Literature Regarding the Mechanical Injury of Fish in Spillways and Stilling Basins*. Report to the U.S. Army Corps of Engineers, Portland District, Portland, Oregon.

Turnpenny, A. 1998. "Mechanisms of Fish Damage in Low-Head Turbines: An Experimental Appraisal." In: *Fish Migration and Bypasses*. M. Jungwirth, S. Schmutz, and S. Weiss (eds.), Fisheries News Books, London, England.

Turnpenny, A.W.H., M. H. Davis, J. M. Fleming, and J. K. Davies. 1992. Experimental Studies Relating to the Passage of Fish and Shrimps Through Tidal Power Turbines. National Power PLC, Fawley, Hampshire, United Kingdom.

Wittinger, R., J. Ferguson, and T. Carlson. 1995. *Proceedings, Turbine Fish Passage Survival Workshop*. Report to the U.S. Army Corps of Engineers, North Pacific Division, Portland, Oregon.